ISBN 978-0-243-51937-8
PIBN 10802927

1 MONTH OF
FREE
READING

at
www.ForgottenBooks.com

By purchasing this book you are eligible for one month membership to ForgottenBooks.com, giving you unlimited access to our entire collection of over 700,000 titles via our web site and mobile apps.

To claim your free month visit:
www.forgottenbooks.com/free802927

ASPECT AND INFLUENCE

OF

CHRISTIANITY

UPON THE

COMMERCIAL CHARACTER:

A DISCOURSE,

DELIVERED AT MONTREAL, OCTOBER 15, 1837.

BY THE

Rev. NEWTON BOSWORTH, F. R. A. S.

MONTREAL :

WILLIAM GREIG, 195, ST. PAUL STREET;

AND LESSLIE & SONS, TORONTO.

CAMPBELL AND BECKET, PRINTERS, PLACE D'ARMES.

PREFACE.

It was thought, by some friends who heard the substance of the following Discourse, that its publication might be useful at the present crisis. In a single address of ordinary length, it was quite impossible to discuss, with adequate fulness, the important topics it embraces. The writer considers it as only a collection of hints; of such hints, however, as he deemed important, and likely, by the blessing of God, to lead to a higher object than the pursuit of any transient good. He wished, as a minister of religion, to lead his hearers, as he now desires to lead his readers, to a consideration of their " latter end," and the means of obtaining " durable riches, righteousness," and eternal life. Should this object be attained, if it be only in a single instance, he will have reason to bless God that he was led first to deliver, and then to print, this plain discourse. He would express his conviction that a more extended view of the subject, in both its divisions, by any one of competent abilities and leisure, would have a tendency to produce lasting and extensive good. He is persuaded that the transactions of Commerce are often conducted on principles at variance with those of the Gospel, and that those who thus pursue it are in great danger of losing the unseen and eternal in their disproportionate attention to the visible and temporary. May the Author of all good smile upon this attempt to avert so unspeakable an evil.

Montreal, November 8, 1837.

a
s
o

Godliness is profitable unto all things.

It is one among the numerous excellencies of Christianity that it meets man in every condition, and adapts itself with astonishing facility to his circumstances and his wants, whatever may be the diversity of the one or the extent of the other. It is scarcely, if at all, possible for the most lively imagination to picture a state or emergency in which a human being can be placed on earth, where some part or other of God's holy word can be of no advantage to him. There is no sorrow that it cannot alleviate, no enquiry which it cannot practically answer, no principle which it does not illustrate, no motive to seek God and holiness and heaven which it does not suggest, no direction in duty which it does not supply. *The Law of the Lord is perfect, making wise the simple ;* his *statutes are pure, rejoicing the heart ;* his promises are certain, and his salvation is complete to every one that believeth. It is this universal fitness to promote the best interests of our race, this wonderful adaptation to every variety of character, age, condition, and circumstance, that constitutes one of the strongest evidences of the Truth of Revelation, and proves it to have been derived from the Father of Lights, who knew what was *in* man, and what was needful *for* man in this his dependent and probationary state.

The term *Godliness* in the text, though in its more general acceptation expressive of likeness to God, or conformity to his moral character, is applicable in detail to every branch of practical religion. This conformity can only be obtained in the manner, and on the principles, unfolded to us in the Scriptures of truth. The whole contents of the Sacred Volume, as relating to man, may be contemplated under two aspects,—as a Code of Morals, and as a Dispensation of Mercy; the one to prove and regulate his obedience, and the other to point out to him the way of salvation. In both these lights I wish to present the sacred oracles before you in reference to the subject which is to engage our consideration, and to shew their influence in the formation of that *godliness* which *is profitable unto all things, having the promise of the life that now is, and of that which is to come;* contributing as effectively to our real welfare in the present state as to our preparation for the bliss of eternity.

I. As a Code of Morals, the system promulgated in the word of God is immeasurably superior to all others that the world has ever seen. Those who have compared it with the dictates and prescriptions of heathen morality, are fully convinced of this fact: even infidels themselves have confessed that the latter are not to be compared to the morality of the Gospel. *Their rock is not as our rock, even our enemies themselves being judges.* The mind of man is both too impure and too ignorant to relish or to discover principles so holy, and precepts so admirable, as those which Christianity developes. It will not be expected, on this occasion, that I should traverse the wide field of Christian obedience, and shew how every part of it is affected by the precepts of the Gospel, or even that I should state at length the grounds of moral obligations: it will be sufficient to shew the bearing of scriptural injunction upon the commercial character, and its tendency, when faithfully obeyed, to produce the most substantial benefits.

The advantages of Commerce are manifold and obvious. It promotes the intercourse of nations,—enlarges the boundaries of knowledge,—contributes to the welfare of mankind by an interchange of commodities, supplying the wants of one country by the excess of another,—calls into action the energies of the bold, the skilful, and the enterprizing,—and, what in the estimate of the Christian philanthropist constitutes its highest excellence, it opens facilities for the introduction of the Gospel into all lands and nations.

To ensure success, on Scriptural principles, in the pursuits of commerce, Integrity, Diligence, and

Moderation are indispensably requisite, whatsoever other qualities, as adjuncts or modifications of these, may be included in our principles of action. Now these are all either enjoined by direct precept, or inculcated in some other form, in the moral code of the Sacred Scriptures.

1. INTEGRITY. This fundamental principle,—comprehending in its wide extent fidelity to engagements, punctuality in the discharge of obligations, fairness in dealing, "a just weight and full measure," accuracy in report, and universal equity in all its modes and ramifications,—is enjoined by the word of God in a great variety of forms, both preceptive and exemplary. To quote them would be an endless task, and unnecessary to those who are acquainted with the morality of the Bible. Perhaps the essence of them all is embodied in this divine aphorism of our Great Teacher, *All things whatsoever ye would that men should do to you, do you even so to them ; for this is the law.* Were this most admirable rule universally acted upon, it would banish for ever that crooked policy which vitiates the purity of commercial intercourse, and introduces interminable jealousies, suspicions, and discords among men, even in the ordinary transactions of life. By the strict observance of this rule a person would acquire the confidence of the community in which he dwelt, and a character for "integrity and uprightness," which would contribute materially to his success ; a success, of which the value would be enhanced by the consciousness of having done "the thing that is right." Of such a man it may be said, with the utmost truth

and emphasis, that "his word is his bond;" and if the customs of society, the uncertainty of life, and the frailty of memory did not require it, the form of a written security might in his case be dispensed with. How different from him whose word can never be relied upon, whose representations are received with distrust, whose promises are never confided in, and who, by a series of petty shifts and evasions, or of fraudulent transactions on a more extended scale, acquires for himself the disgraceful notoriety of an unfair trader. The one is a blessing to society, the other a curse; the one inspires confidence, the other destroys it; the one diffuses a beneficial, the other a baneful, influence all around him; the one is honest and open as the day, the other dark and suspicious as the night; by the one the true honour and dignity of the mercantile character is sustained, by the other it is brought into discredit and contempt.

Upon my younger hearers I would urge, with all the earnestness of which I am capable, an immediate attention to the importance of unbending integrity as an essential ingredient in the formation of character. Let them adopt it, at once and for ever, as the foundation principle of all their doings. Let it enter among their first conceptions of the qualities indispensable for their future guidance. Let them cherish it as a precious germ which shall evolve and expand itself in virtuous action. Let it become an element in all their thoughts and feelings, until they acquire such a habit of "doing justly" that it shall be painful and unnatural for them to act in a contrary manner. Thus

2. DILIGENCE. This also is emphatically recommended in the Sacred Directory, both by precept and example. *The desire of the slothful killeth him. Be thou diligent to know the state of thy flocks, and look well to thy herds. The hand of the diligent maketh rich. Seest thou a man diligent in his business? He shall stand before kings;* intimating that, according to the established laws of social life, industry in our proper calling is the most effectual way of attaining success and respectability in our secular pursuits. This is a comprehensive direction, enjoining not only activity, but perseverance; prompting not merely to an occasional act, but to a *habit* of attention and labour. No extensive purpose can be accomplished, and no great object can be obtained, by fitful and transient efforts, however intense; but by continued and patient application. This, while it is one of the most useful of all habits, is comparatively rare; being by no means of easy acquisition. The most ardent and energetic are the most exposed to failure in this point. They seize upon an object with avidity, amuse themselves with it for a while, and then are urged, by desire of change or love of novelty, to relinquish it in favour of some new pursuit. They enter upon an employment

which strikes their fancy with delight, and fills their hearts with promise ; but it soon becomes irksome to them by its sameness, or discouraging by little difficulties in the way, real or imaginary, and they retire from it in despair. Having heard the history of one and another who have risen to opulence by successful engagements in trade, they are naturally desirous of proceeding in the same course, at least of reaping the same reward. But here they deceive themselves : they are dazzled and attracted by the result, but overlook the means which lead to it ; or, after a brief trial, take umbrage at the pains and labours which are the indispensable conditions of success.

Now this state of mind must be resolutely opposed and overcome, or all expectations of success from the pursuit of business will end in disappointment. Let, then, the whole subject, in all its tendencies, bearings, and requirements be carefully and deliberately weighed, and the decision be made accordingly. Let a determination be formed and acted upon to give close and unremitted attention to the object, in its minute details as well as its larger departments, during all the time allotted to the purpose ; and let there be added, to the energy which excites to action, the diligence necessary to render it effective, and the unconquerable perseverance which shall carry it onward to its desired consummation.

In the next place, the Scriptures require us to exercise

3. MODERATION in the pursuit of earthly good.

They do this, in passages too numerous to be quoted, not only by the authority of the universal sovereign, but by assigning reasons for the injunction ; and reasons, too, so clear and powerful that those who refuse obedience, are chargeable with not only opposing the prerogative, but calling into question the wisdom, of the Most High. *Let your moderation be known unto all men,*—so constantly practised, and so visibly displayed, that none may have cause to charge you with departing from it. *He that maketh haste to be rich shall not be innocent.* This declaration, though made by the wisest of men, is not, I am aware, in unison with the too prevalent spirit of the present age. Like some of the instructions of our Lord, it will be deemed a " hard saying ;" but it is nevertheless founded on the nature of things, and enforced by the authority of Divine Inspiration. A too eager desire of acquisition blinds the understanding to the distinction between right and wrong, and betrays the heart into an indifference as to the measures to be pursued, or into an adoption, without scruple, of such as are manifestly evil. The Apostle Paul, in his first Epistle to Timothy, looking at the same principle in another form, observes, *They that will be rich fall into temptation and a snare, and into many foolish and hurtful lusts, which drown men in destruction and perdition,* and declares that those who have indulged to excess the *love of money, have pierced themselves through with many sorrows.* This *determination* to be rich, at all hazards and by any means, whether conscience be wounded or not, is no less likely than the passionate *haste* censured by Solomon to lead to a violation of justice and truth ; and when both are united, and exert their powers in combination, nothing else can be expected than an utter disregard of the precepts of morality, the claims of benevolence, and the fear of God. A selfish concern for his own personal safety may have led the unhappy subject of this passion to be cautious not to offend against the letter of human laws ; but no other semblance of regard to honour or to virtue can be expected from him, or is to be discovered in his practice.

The rapacious spirit of modern commerce, having thrown off all moral restraint, is prepared for every species of dishonourable artifice, and therefore adopts, without reluctance or hesitation, measures of the most unjustifiable character, regardless alike of the property or the lives of others. It is as cruel as it is undis- criminating. The only question is, whether the gain which is sought, be it just or unjust, is likely to be obtained. All other considerations are thrown to the winds. Shame is absent, and conscience is asleep. We need not travel far for examples of this unprincipled rapacity. Some of our own traders—I am ashamed to avow it—in their dealings with the Indians, not only purchased their valuable articles for very trifling and inferior considerations, but by the intro- duction of ardent spirits among them, to inebriate and deceive them, have inflicted upon them a lasting injury, which centuries will be insufficient to remove. To such a height had this abomination ascended, that it was found necessary to restrain it by authority. The North West Company, much to their honour, have

B

opposed the introduction of intoxicating liquors among the Indians, and have excluded it from all those sections of the country where they have exclusive control over the trade. The influence of this regulation has already proved highly salutary, in the improved conduct of the Indians, and the increased safety of travelling among them. The Legislature of Upper Canada has also enacted a law forbidding the use of ardent spirits by our traders among the Indians, whether by sale, or gift, or any other manner whatsoever. By that practice, thus at last abolished, we have debased, and degraded, and well nigh exterminated the aboriginal inhabitants of this land, who might, by kind treatment and Christian instruction, have been moulded into a noble and virtuous population.

The eager desire to amass wealth, and the determination to do so, without regard to means, has been productive of another evil which requires to be noticed,—the careless exposure of borrowed capital. When a zealous votary of Mammon, after exhausting his own resources, is either compelled by difficulty, or tempted by hope, to avail himself of the aid of borrowed money, it not unfrequently happens that he engages in more hazardous speculations, and with greater temerity than before. Instead of being more cautious, he is less so, because he has greater means at command; and being eager to redeem himself, or rapidly to acquire a fortune, he fails perhaps in both objects, and loses all. This is a " sore evil," and a most censurable practice. Whatever right a man may claim to do what he will with his own, he has none to involve another in his ruin, or to risque the property which he obtained on loan, except upon the most clear and rational prospect of success. But this recklessness of consequences, this dereliction of prudence and honour, though in these days too common to excite wonder, will admit of no justification in the court of conscience. *He that maketh haste to be rich shall not be innocent.*

But this is not all. When the object is more cautiously and steadily pursued, it is often permitted so completely to absorb the whole soul, and keep the faculties upon the stretch, that there is neither time, nor desire, nor energy left for mental improvement, or attention to the claims of religion and the soul. If the plain and humble Christian who has no time to read any thing but his Bible, may be denominated, in a good sense of the words, *a man of one book*, he who is thus confined to earthly pursuits, may be as justly termed, in a bad sense, *a man of one idea*. He thinks of nothing but accumulation ; and however magnificent the idea may be in his own conception, he cannot, by all his efforts, expand it beyond the magnitude of a bubble which rolls upon the earth and bursts at his feet, or floats in the lower stratum of the atmosphere till it is lost in air. Engaged in one unceasing round of worldly occupation, the wretched slave of avarice has but little reason to congratulate himself on any superiority to his sable brethren who labour in the mine or at the oar, in the misery of constrained servitude, and the degradation of mental darkness. Constantly panting after gain, and exclaiming, *Give, give,* he never says, *It is enough*, and never enjoys what he thus laboriously acquires. What greater calamity can befal a rational being than to be fast bound in the chains of a never satisfied cupidity?

It is to a violation of this rule of moderately pursuing our secular concerns, that we are to ascribe, if I mistake not, the sad disaster which has recently convulsed the commercial world from its centre to its extremities, involving thousands in ruin, and shaking the confidence of nations. To this we may ascribe the passion for over-trading, and adventurous speculation beyond the bounds of prudence and probability; the production of factitious capital, which, resting on spurious credit, is liable to be dissipated with that which supports it; the disregard of all the rules and calculations of better times; the scornful rejection of those slower but more certain methods which made our forefathers respectable and happy; and the consequent adoption of wild, chimerical, and unlawful measures, equally at variance with discretion and morality.

It is a remarkable circumstance in the history of the late transactions, that no loss of real property can be assigned as the cause of the universal distress which has prevailed, and which all classes of the community so strongly feel. No famine has visited any considerable portion of the globe; no pestilence has destroyed the race of serviceable animals; no inundation has carried off millions of acres of produce, ready for the reaper's hand; no tempest has wrecked and destroyed a fleet of merchantmen, with all their valuable cargo; no hurricane has swept over country after country to desolate the earth; no volcano has sent forth its fires to such an extent as to reduce the inhabitants of a continent to poverty; no earthquake has swallowed a hundred trading cities with all their well stored repositories of food, clothing, and merchandize; no general* conflagration has reduced to smoke and ashes the materials of commerce and the supply of human wants. We hear not any complaints of deficiency in the usual articles of consumption and merchandize. Commodities of every kind are every where to be found; the only difficulty is to obtain and pay for them. Providence has been very bountiful to us; but *in the midst of* our *sufficiency* we *are in straits.* How is this to be accounted for? Evidently by a derangement of that artificial and delusive system which a morbid craving of accumulation, and a neglect of moral considerations, have introduced into the commercial world. Illustrations and proofs of this sentiment might be easily adduced, did the time and place permit.

In this point of our enquiry, then, it is of great importance to observe that the eternal Sovereign will not suffer his laws to be broken with impunity, whether they be the laws of our physical constitution— of our social intercourse—of our moral relations—or of his spiritual kingdom. If we thrust our hand into

* I do not overlook the great fire at New York last year. It destroyed much property, ruined many individuals, and put a transient stop in some quarters to the operations of trade; but it does not invalidate the substantial truth of the statement, as it will not account for a thousandth part of the misery which the world has suffered, is suffering, and will suffer

the fire, we cannot avoid feeling pain ; if we practise intemperance, we injure our health ; if we wish to have friends we must shew ourselves friendly ; if we infringe upon the rights of others we must suffer in our own ; if we violate the dictates of conscience in our dealings with each other, *that* conscience will, sooner or later, require an ample compensation for the insult. The laws that should regulate this intercourse are plainly laid down in Scripture, and some of them have now been pointed out to you ; and never will nations, communities, and I may add, individuals, be secure from the danger of such disasters as have recently overtaken us till the principles of those laws are generally adopted.

It is in the social community as in the world of nature. The operation and observance of the immutable laws enacted by the great Creator is essential to the intended effect ; the neglect or violation of those laws is as necessarily productive of failure or disappointment. If the action of gravity were suspended, or any of the original forces disturbed which retain the planets in their orbits, confusion, irregularity, or destruction would ensue to the general system. If in the vegetable world a plant should fade and die before its fruit has been matured, we infer that at some point the established order of vegetation has been deranged, either by defect of nutriment, or injury of structure. So, in human affairs, to set at nought the plain and settled laws of action, will be to endanger all hope of success, and frustrate the design by the very effort to secure it.

A character formed on the principles, and according to the model, distinctly laid down by divine authority, may be expected to exhibit such qualities as the following. The person possessing it would maintain a strict integrity in all his concerns, making his engagements with caution, and fulfilling them with scrupulous fidelity. He would take no mean advantage of any favourable circumstances in which he might be placed; but, while he would call his skill into exercise to take every honest advantage of their occurrence, he would remember the claims of equity and honour. His wishes for himself would regulate his treatment of others. The duties of his vocation he would discharge with unremitting assiduity, and its objects he would pursue with diligent activity, yet with calm perseverance, so moderating his attention to them as to *possess his soul in patience.* He would be careful not so to entangle himself with a multiplicity and diversity of concerns as to perplex and fetter his mind; but reserve himself for such other occupations as duty or inclination call for. Against that feverish anxiety which results from rash and hazardous speculations he would be especially on his guard. Remembering that a man's life and happiness consist not *in the abundance of the things which he possesseth,* he would seek to use as well as to appropriate, to enjoy as well as to obtain. A safe and moderate competency being the point at which he aimed, he would cheerfully devote to the attainment of it as much time as it required; but would not suffer it to encroach upon other purposes, in his estimation at least equally valuable. The cultivation of the nobler faculties of

his nature, the improvement of his mind, the enlarge-
ment of his knowledge, the pleasure of social
intercourse and of benevolent exertion, would receive
a competent portion of his regard ; and jealously would
he resist any abridgement of the hours allotted
to these engagements. Regarding *every thing* as
beautiful in its season, he would assign to business and
to recreation their just and equitable portions ; and,
by this agreeable interchange of employments, at once
promote his cheerfulness and health, and check that
tendency to avarice which an exclusive pursuit of gain
never fails to produce. Holding thus the balance
even, wisely dividing his attention, repelling extrava-
gant desires, seeking only the practicable and the safe,
studying *whatsoever things are honest, true, and of
good report*, he would most effectually secure his own
interest and peace of mind, while he displayed an
example which, if universally imitated, would equally
advance the general good.

Happily, this is not altogether a hypothetical
portrait, or a solitary instance of worth ; numerous
examples of it exist on both sides of the Atlantic ; but
they are too rare. Had they been general, instead of
partial,—forming the rule rather than the exception,—
wild speculation, reckless adventure, unprincipled
rapacity would never have risen to so fearful a
predominance, and the greater part of the calamities
that have recently overtaken us would have been
unheard of and unknown. Fewer rapid fortunes might
have been made, but the general prosperity of nations
would have been placed on a firmer basis.

Such solid virtues as have been referred to, are best favoured and cherished by adhering to the maxims of Holy writ; and Divine Providence generally blesses them with success and reputation. Even so distant and feeble an approximation to his own infinite excellence the Kings of kings *delighteth to honour*.

Thus, then, it appears that Godliness, by the principles it inculcates, and the practices it enjoins, is eminently favourable to the temporal interests of mankind at large, and that the Bible, as a Code of Morals, is worthy of perpetual and universal regard.

But these precepts, excellent as they must be deemed by every considerate and well-ordered mind, may be observed from very insufficient and unworthy motives. Adapted as they are to promote individual and general benefit, they may be resorted to for that very end, and that alone; from a mere principle of selfishness, without the slightest regard to the authority which enjoined them. A thoughtful and observant man, reflecting on the tendencies of human action, and learning wisdom from the experience of others, is directly led to the conclusion that " Honesty is the best policy," and that the safest way of obtaining an object is to pursue it cautiously and laboriously; and this conviction falling in with his natural temperament, he resolves to act with integrity, and to manage all his affairs with diligence and moderation. He adopts the plan, pursues it, and prospers. To such a one, we may say—' You have gained your object, but you have failed in your duty, because you *gave not God the glory.*

You have acted upon principles, thus far *according to godliness,* but as you did not adopt them from a holy motive, they will only condemn you at the bar of judgment. You have gathered around you many comforts, but none that will comfort your spirit when it is departing into eternity. You have acquired a respectable standing in society, but how do you stand in the sight of God? Slander has not breathed upon your reputation, nor suspicion even cast a glance upon your honour; but you have loved the world, and sought not the honour that cometh from above. You have been faithful to your engagements, you have exercised the courtesies of life, you have not betrayed your friend, you have not oppressed the poor—but you have loved the world. The miserable you have often pitied and relieved, from the promptings of natural sympathy; the welfare of your country you have advanced, on the dictates of enlightened patriotism; but you have loved the world; and love it still; it is your chosen portion, and you desire no better. Now *if any man love the world, the love of the Father is not in him.* You have failed, then, in the very first principle of duty towards your Maker and Judge. *The first and great commandment is, Thou shalt love the Lord thy God with all thy heart, with all thy mind, with all thy soul, and with all thy strength.* This commandment you have broken. To you may be addressed the awful words of our Lord to the unbelieving Jews, *I know you, that you have not the love of God in you.* And he knows you, too, as thoroughly and as intimately as he knew them; and he knows that the solemn charge is as applicable to you as it was to them. The love of the world has so completely filled your heart, that there is no room in it for *the habitation of God through the spirit.* Nor do you desire that He should dwell there. The Law of God is unchangeable, and cannot be revoked. It will not admit of the least deviation from its requirements, because it is *perfect,* like its Divine Author. But this law you have broken; and you have no means, in yourself, of repairing it, or of satisfying its demands. The sentence of condemnation is gone forth against you; and the sword of eternal justice is drawn to execute it upon you. If you die in this state, you will *l'e down in darkness,* and perish under the frown of the Almighty;

To such a character as I have supposed (O! that it were only supposition, and not reality) it would be my duty to address these alarming declarations, to warn, rebuke, and exhort him to *flee from the wrath to come.* But is there any hope? Blessed be God, there is; and it is to be found in the Gospel of Christ. There let us search for it, while we consider the Sacred Oracles as proclaiming to us,

II. A DISPENSATION OF MERCY. Man is not now in his original condition. God created him " upright" and holy. He stood high in the favour of his Maker, whose presence he enjoyed, and in whose service he delighted. His residence was Eden, and every action was piety and pleasure. He was placed under a law, with but one prohibition, as a mark of his dependence, and a test of his faithfulness. But this prohibition he broke through ; and thus renounced his allegiance, forfeited his peace, exposed himself to the just anger of his righteous sovereign, and involved himself and his posterity in misery and ruin. Sentence of condemnation was passed upon him, and expulsion from paradise ensued. But *God, who is rich in mercy*, looked with pity on his wretched and guilty creature, devised a plan for his restoration to happiness and purity, without any compromise of his dignity or impeachment of his rectitude. A Saviour was announced ; and *in due time Christ died for the ungodly*, that *all who believe in him should not perish*, as for their disobedience they deserved to do, but receive the pardon of their sins, and *have eternal life.*

Law, in itself, knows nothing of mercy. Its jurisdiction is separate and independent. It makes no provision for the breach of its own enactments. It is absolute and inflexible in its demands. The decrees of human legislation are, indeed, sometimes repealed or their infraction connived at, because they are found to be inefficient, unjust, or impracticable ; but the law of God is *holy, and just, and good*, a transcript of his own eternal rectitude ; and therefore to pass over a transgression of it, without an adequate recompence of some sort, would be in itself an infringement of equity. As obedience is due to the great governor of the universe, to disobey is to rob him of his right, and to tolerate disobedience is to encourage rebellion, and disturb the equity of the divine administration. *Sin is a transgression of the law ;* and every sinner, if he offend but in one point, sets at nought the divine authority, and exposes himself to the penalty of death, and exclusion from heavenly blessedness.

The Scriptures assure us that *we are all by nature the children of wrath,* that we have *all erred and strayed from* the way of God, and that *sentence is passed upon all men, for that all have sinned.* But a reference to sin in general is little likely to work in your minds the conviction that you are in a state of condemnation, since men are singularly ingenious in finding excuses for their crimes, and persuading themselves that all is well with them, even when they are most obnoxious to the divine displeasure. I shall, therefore, endeavour to fix your attention upon that particular offence to which the pursuits of commerce more especially expose you, though in truth every human being, more or less, is liable and prone to it. I mean the love of the world, and the choice of it as a portion, to the exclusion of the Infinite good. Ever since the fall there has been a fatal propensity in man to forsake God, to love, and even *worship, the creature more than the Creator,* to substitute the pleasures of sense for those of reason, and the gratification of the passions for the favour of the Almighty. Of two great evils the whole human race have been guilty—*forsaking the fountain of living waters,* and *hewing out cisterns that can hold no water.* Nor can any of you plead exemption from the charge. If, then, while engaged in your lawful calling, you pursue the things of the world in the spirit of the world; if your motives are purely selfish, beginning and terminating in your personal gratification; if, when you prosper in your designs, you assume all the credit to yourself, and give not to God *the honour due unto his name,* or when riches increase you *set your heart upon them ;* if you are looking to the present state as your rest, and not desiring or preparing for a better ; if you have given your heart to vanity and not to God, and are living to yourselves and not to Him ; if you deny yourselves in nothing because he has forbidden it, and perform no action from a design to please him and a regard for his authority ;—then are you in a condition which angels regard with pity, and fiends with malignant joy. You are guilty of a wilful violation of the First and Great commandment, and liable to all the penalties denounced against it,—for you love not God *with all your heart.*

To whatever subterfuge you may have recourse, and whatever palliations you may offer, you cannot escape from the charge, while the law of God stands unrepealed, and his equitable character as governor of the universe remains unchanged. Both stand out against you in terrible array : and unless they be withdrawn, you have nothing to expect but the execution of the sentence, and nothing before you but a *fearful looking-for of judgment and of fiery indignation.* What plea can you advance in arrest of judgment? Will you say that, convinced of your error and your guilt, you will for ever renounce and abandon them both? With whatever sincerity you may have cherished this idea, it will not avail to extricate you from danger. God *requireth that which is past.* He cannot renounce his holiness, or suffer *one tittle of his law to fail.* All analogy, as well as all justice, is against you in this matter. A resolution not to contract a future debt will not discharge an old one ; a determination not to repeat an offence will never compensate for one that has been already committed. Injury has been done, and you cannot repair it ; guilt has been contracted, and you cannot remove it. Could you, from this hour, keep the whole law of God in all its purity, without any deviation or defect, with internal affection as well as external conformity, you would have no superfluity of merit to fill up the measure of deficient obedience. The position, then, in which you stand as a sinner before God, viewed from whatever point it may, is the most fearful and affecting that imagination can conceive. The law says, " Do this, and thou shalt live. Transgress this, and thou shalt die." The rewards of obedience you cannot claim, for you have not rendered it ; the defects of obedience you cannot supply, for you have no resource to draw from, and you are continually adding to their number ; the penalties of disobedience you cannot escape, for you have incurred them ; for the sin of disobedience you cannot atone, since you have no compensation to propose, and no offering to present.

Happily man is not left without hope, under all the pressure of this misery and guilt. The Gospel, as an angel of mercy, comes in to his relief ; and herein consists its superlative value. *Glad tidings of great joy* are brought to those who are lying under the curse of a violated law. The God of love beholds with compassion his degraded and perishing creature, and says, *Deliver him from going down to the pit, for I have found a ransom.* The offended party provides means of reconciliation for his offending child. *Herein is love, not that we loved God, but that he loved us, and sent his son to be the propitiation for our sins.* The Saviour himself, gladly co-operating in the covenant of peace, flies to our rescue; and, laying aside his glory, steps down from the throne, and *humbles himself* to the *death of the cross.* The Gospel announces this astonishing plan in all the freeness and fulness of its provisions, and proclaims pardon through the blood of the Holy One, by faith in his name. Thus mercy and truth are united with righteousness and peace. Thus the claims of justice are secured by the very act in which the Divine benignity is exercised, while God's glory is promoted, and the sinner eternally saved.

You will perceive, my brethren, at one view, the practical application of these cheering truths, and learn that as the law, by the penalties it denounces upon transgression of which all are guilty, is a ministration of death, so the gospel, by the deliverance it promises and secures, is a ministration of life. The one destroys, because men have failed in their obedience; the other saves, because Christ has perfectly fulfilled the law in our behalf, and suffered the penalties which sinners have deserved. But to whom are these benefits available? *To every one that believeth.* If, therefore, my brethren, under a sense of guilt and a feeling of danger, you apply to the Redeemer; if, humbled, broken-hearted, penitent, you come to him who alone can exalt and comfort you ; if you renounce your own imperfect righteousness as a ground of confidence before God, and put on the righteousness of Christ, *even the righteousness which is of God by faith ;* if, persuaded that you must sink and be lost without divine aid, you cry out ' *Save, Lord, or we perish ;*' if you thus *behold* by faith *the Lamb of God*, trust in his atoning blood, rely on his all-perfect sacrifice, obedience, and advocacy, and in this manner *come unto God by Him*,—you have the most absolute promise that a Deity can give, of acceptance, pardon, and salvation ; for whosoever thus seeks an entrance into his kingdom and glory shall *in no wise be cast out.*

But if, on the other hand, you are so careless of your eternal interests that you have no concern about them ; or if the world has gained such an ascendancy over you that you are unwilling to renounce it even for salvation itself ; or if you are too proud to be indebted to another for those blessings which you fancy your own virtues deserve ; the Gospel will be no " dispensation of mercy" to you. For you, Christ will have *died in vain,* while you thus contemptuously reject his mercy, and in the most awful manner thus *judge yourselves unworthy of eternal life.*

And for what does the votary of the world forego these high advantages ? What potent influence can have lulled him into a forgetfulness of his eternal interests ? It is the *deceitfulness of sin ;* the benumbing power of selfishness on a depraved heart ; the predominance of worldly motives in a worldly spirit.

D

In matters of commerce the invariable object is profit, each party seeking to obtain that which to him respectively is of more value than that which he parts with ; and he who gives an exorbitant price for an inferior commodity, or barters a rare jewel for a thing of nought, is justly chargeable with folly, and deemed incompetent to manage even the most ordinary affairs. It is some consolation, amidst the losses of trade, to know that their extent may be calculated, and by diligence and attention sometimes repaired. But who can calculate the loss of heavenly blessedness, and who can regain it when once the sentence is pronounced, and *the door is shut?* The *redemption of the soul is precious ;* but if it be not secured in the present life, *it ceaseth for ever.* We naturally look with surprise and censure upon him who lavishes his fortune upon trifles, or sacrifices the welfare of a whole life for the pleasure of a moment; but he who prefers the gratifications of sense to the favour of God, and loses his soul rather than give up his sin, is guilty of an infatuation for which language has no name, and which nothing can account for but the melancholy fact that the God of this world *hath blinded his eyes,* and hardened his heart.

There was one of old who contented himself with making provision for the flesh *to fulfil the lusts thereof,* and whose whole pleasure consisted in accumulation, and in plans to secure what he had gained, to whom it was said, *Thou fool! this night thy soul shall be required of thee : then whose shall those things be that thou hast provided?* Then, where shall that soul be,

which thus limits its desires to a perishing world,—
thus prostitutes its noble faculties to the pampering of
the flesh,—thus wraps up its energies in the narrow
circle of selfish indulgence,—thus hangs its eternal
destinies on a thread so slender as mortal existence?

Suffer me, my brethren, to press upon you the all-
important question, How stands the matter, then,
between God and your souls? Do you think of every
thing but Him, and his righteous commands? Are
you satisfied if your worldly designs prosper, without
feeling any concern whether happiness or misery be
your portion in eternity? Is the frown or the smile of
your Creator and Judge, a matter of equal indifference
to you? Is it your pleasure to live *without God in the
world*, and while you remember with gratitude every
other benefactor, to forget Him who gave you being?
Have you no love to the Saviour, no delight in his
service, no desire to be like him, no hope to be with
him? Is this world *all* in your esteem, and the future
nothing?

When you consider the mutable nature of all earthly
good,—its limited power to satisfy the best desires of
the soul, or rather its utter insufficiency for this end,—
and above all the transient possession we have of it,
for *we brought nothing into this world, and it is certain
we can carry nothing out,*—you will at once perceive
the wisdom of seeking *a more enduring substance*, of
laying up *treasure in heaven*, of securing a title to an
inheritance that is *incorruptible, undefiled, and fadeth
not away.* You surely need no argument to prove to

you the absurdity of that unhappy man's determination who said, " Soul, take thine ease ; thou hast much goods laid up for many years." What is there in barns, and fruits, and worldly abundance to give " ease" to the soul, when God *requires it ?* These things have their use, and our Heavenly Father knoweth that we have *need* of them, during our sojourn upon earth ; but they are only adapted to the wants of the body,— the soul requires a more ethereal nutriment, and can be happy only in God. To be alienated from Him is to be severed from the only source of true felicity ; to be an enemy to Him is to be at enmity with our own peace. To be reconciled to Him is our highest privilege and dignity ; to enjoy Him is to enjoy every thing. Behold, then, another illustration of the doctrine of the text, that *Godliness is profitable unto all things, having the promise of the life that now is, and of that which is to come.*

The annals of commerce are not destitute of examples tending to evince the same truth. Many names might be adduced of Christian merchants eminent in their generation for piety and wealth, successful in their enterprises, and liberal in their distribution, considering themselves as stewards, not owners, of the property they acquired ; of *men fearing God and hating covetousness,* equally diligent in business, and *fervent in spirit,* serving God in all. Such men give a tone an. an influence to the society in which they move, and are an honour to the profession in which they are engaged. They have shewn the compatibility of an active life with a Christian spirit, and have taught us how to *live unto God* while living among men. With all their other acquisitions, they have obtained the *pearl of great price :* with a competency of worldly good, they are also *rich in faith,* and *heirs of the kingdom.* Walking in all humility before God, and enjoying the comforts of his love, they have at the same time acquired the confidence and respect of all who are judges of character and lovers of true worth. They are *not ashamed of the Gospel of Christ.* On the contrary they glory in it, and are careful, by the consistency and holiness of their deportment, to *adorn the doctrine of God their Saviour.* Of a similar spirit, I trust, are some who now hear me. May their example be universally imitated, and diffuse its holy influence throughout the whole community.

Suffer me to conclude with a few words of exhortation.

First. *Be upon your guard against the love of the world.* Nothing is more destructive to the souls of men. It is the universal temptation which besets the human race ; and nothing but the grace of God can deliver you from it. There is no danger against which the Saviour and his Apostles are more frequent and solemn in their warnings than this ; and the reason is obvious,—there is none to which we are more exposed, or which is more successful in its attacks and more fatal in its consequences. From the carnal mind it will receive a warm and cordial welcome, as in perfect harmony with its propensities and desires ; and upon such a mind it will exert its deadly power till it is plunged beyond hope into the pit of perdition. Even the Christian is not exempt from its influence. It makes its approaches in so insidious a manner, and comes in such a specious guise, under such alluring names, and with such delusive pretensions and promises, that even the *children of light* are liable to be deceived by it. Should it gain an ascendancy in your hearts, it will mar your comfort, cloud your evidences, lower your spirituality, impede your usefulness, and make work for bitter repentance. Watch against it, therefore, my beloved brethren, I beseech you, with incessant vigilance, and pray against it with a holy importunity, that the power of Christ may rest upon you, and bring your very thoughts into a sweet subjection to his will.

Secondly. *Be careful that you mistake not the way of salvation.* Some of you may have been more correct and moral in your deportment than others, and on that account may deem yourselves in a fair way for heaven. But trust not to your own virtues, which are very imperfect at the best, and very deficient at the utmost. If they spring from any other motive than the love of God, they are not virtues in His sight, whatever they may appear in your's. If *weighed in the balance*, they will all *be found wanting*. The very best of them will *not stand in the judgment*, much less atone for the sins you have committed. Your own hearts will condemn you. *By the deeds of the law shall no flesh living be justified ;* and if not justified before God, you cannot be saved. The blood of Christ alone will avail you here. It was shed for the guilty, and every one that believeth in him shall receive the benefit of his death, the pardon of sin, and everlasting life. Those who do not receive Christ by faith—a faith which works by love, and shews its reality by the fruits of holiness which it bears—remain under the law, exposed to its penalties, and awaiting its curse. *There is no other name given under heaven by which we can be saved ;* but *that* name is all-sufficient. His redemption is complete, and presents to the eye of faith all that a guilty sinner needs to set him free from the condemnation of the law, to purify his heart by the influence of the Spirit ; and thus, while it gives a *title* to eternal life, renders him who believes in Jesus, *meet* for the possession and enjoyment of its unutterable blessedness. To renounce his own fancied righteousness is humbling to the pride of man ; but he must be humbled in order to be exalted. Happy those who, like the great Apostle of the Gentiles, desire to appear before the throne, not *having on* their *own righteousness which is of the law, but the righteousness which is of God by faith.* In no other way can heaven be attained. Man cannot earn a right to it— man cannot work a fitness for it. By Christ alone the way is opened—through faith alone we are enabled to walk in that *living way. Thanks be to God for his unspeakable gift.* If you look into yourselves, you will find nothing but matter for despondency ; but if you *look to Jesus,* you behold a foundation strong enough to sustain your hopes to all eternity.

Finally. Whatever my love to your souls may impel me to desire, I am not so presumptious as to suppose that these representations, or any representations that I can make, will prevail upon the sinner to repent and turn to God, or induce the believer to walk more closely with Him, without that divine agency which alone can render them effectual. Paul claimed not this power, either for himself or his eloquent companion and fellow-labourer, Apollos; but still the one continued to plant and the other to water, in the faith that God would give the increase. The Almighty still works by means; and the great means which he has appointed to gather in and edify his church are the exhibition of Christ in the Gospel, and the appeals contained in his holy word. I look to the same all-potent influence on which they rested, to render the gospel to you the *power of God unto salvation*; and *my heart's desire and prayer for you all is, that you may be saved.* Amen.

FINIS.

ERRATA.

Page 10, line 1—read prosperity.

19, 21—*for* call *read* calls.